Tracker Dogs

By Heather Hammonds
Illustrations by Elizabeth Botté

T0342765

Contents

Finding Amy

**by Police Reporter,
Tess Wheeler**

The Millward family has returned home safely, after a family gathering at Forest Reserve Picnic Ground went awry yesterday.

Grave fears were held for the safety of three-year-old Amy. Her parents, John and Margaret, reported she had been sleeping quietly in the shade while the rest of the family played cricket nearby. She was found to be missing when her mother checked on her 15 minutes later.

When the area was searched, Amy's favourite doll was discovered beside a track leading into the bush. With Amy nowhere to be seen, her parents immediately contacted the police.

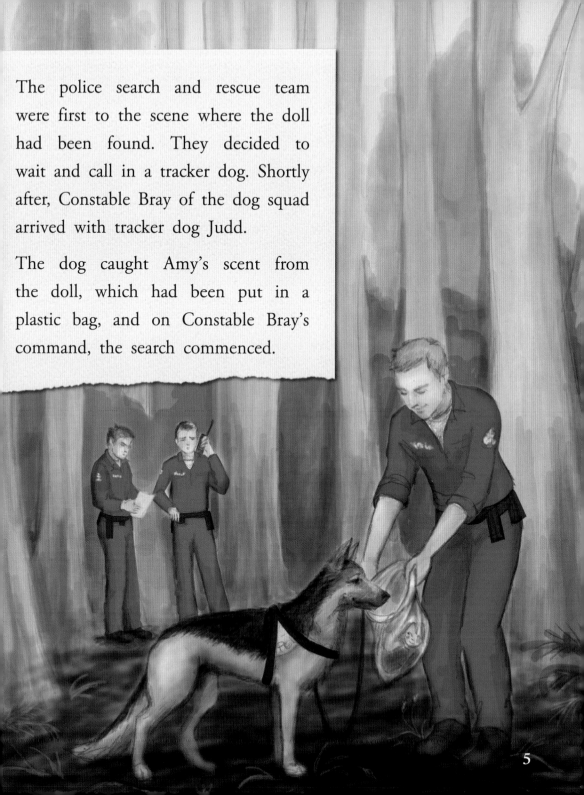

The police search and rescue team were first to the scene where the doll had been found. They decided to wait and call in a tracker dog. Shortly after, Constable Bray of the dog squad arrived with tracker dog Judd.

The dog caught Amy's scent from the doll, which had been put in a plastic bag, and on Constable Bray's command, the search commenced.

At once Judd tracked the scent into the bush, and led the way with the rest of the search team following some distance behind. Unfortunately, after only a few hundred metres, the search ground to a halt. Judd had lost the scent at Fraser's Fire Track. After sniffing the doll again and then sniffing around the area, Judd regained the scent and continued to track the lost child.

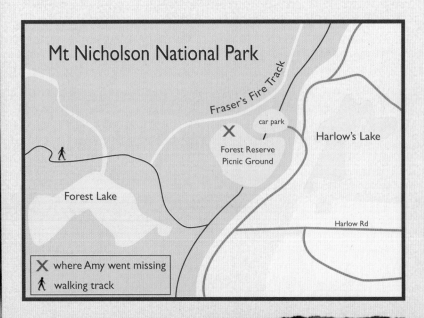

Mt Nicholson National Park

Fraser's Fire Track

car park

Harlow's Lake

Forest Reserve
Picnic Ground

Forest Lake

Harlow Rd

X where Amy went missing

🚶 walking track

Dusk had fallen by the time Amy was eventually located. She had wandered into a gully and, overcome with tiredness, had crawled into a hollow. The search team wrapped her in rescue blankets and carried her back to the Forest Reserve headquarters, where she was attended to by paramedics.

Police held a press conference following Amy's rescue. John Millward praised all involved for their prompt action in mounting the search operation, making particular mention of the tracker dog. "Thanks to the skill of police and the dog squad, we've been quickly reunited with Amy," he said. "We are so thankful that she escaped serious injury, and will always remember the efforts of police dog Judd."

Dogs That Track and Search

All dogs have an excellent sense of smell. Dogs use ten per cent of their brains to identify smells, whereas humans use only one per cent. Wild dogs use their sense of smell to assist them when hunting for food, sniffing out other dogs and smelling danger.

a domestic dog sniffs out a scent

an African hunting dog

It is possible to teach dogs to use their sense of smell to help people in different ways. Some dogs are taught to search for foods or other goods that people are not permitted to take from country to country. They are called detector dogs.

Some dogs are taught to search for missing people. They use their sense of smell to find people lost in bushland. They find disaster victims, too. It takes many months to train dogs to search for victims in rescue situations.

a police dog and its handler search for missing people, following a fire

When a dog is searching for someone, it may be given an article of clothing or something similar that belongs to the person and has been close to their body. The dog can smell the person's scent on the article. The dog is then able to follow this scent to search for the person.

Some police dogs are trained to track and search for suspected criminals. This can be dangerous work for the police dogs and sometimes they are injured in the line of duty.

Tracking is also an exciting dog sport. Many different breeds of dogs are taught to track people and find personal items of clothing, such as socks or hats. Tracking clubs meet at different places. Club members learn how to teach their dogs these skills, and dogs are given rewards at the end of each track.

Most dogs seem to enjoy using their sense of smell to track and search for people and objects. Dogs that track and search have saved many lives, caught many criminals and helped hundreds of tracking club members to have fun.